The Chaotic World
The Dim Field

By

Bernard Benson Sarfo

The Chaotic World

Bernard Benson Sarfo

Published by Bernard Benson Sarfo, 2024.

While every precaution has been taken in the preparation of this book, the publisher assumes no responsibility for errors or omissions, or for damages resulting from the use of the information contained herein.

THE CHAOTIC WORLD

First edition. April 22, 2024.

Copyright © 2024 Bernard Benson Sarfo.

ISBN: 979-8224865475

Written by Bernard Benson Sarfo.

Also by Bernard Benson Sarfo

The Fact Among Facts (1st)
The Fact Among Facts

Standalone
The Youth Murderer
Be Original Not a Copy
The Christians Science or Scholarship
Precious than Paradise
Habit makes future
A shelter from storm and rain
The Science of Life
The Strongest Lion Knockback
The Perfect and Inspiring City
Above Hope, Faith and Love
The Hero's Brave Decisions
The Weakest Among Plants
The Hero's Brave Decisions
Doing Above The Ability
The Wisdom Beyond Power And Greatness

Heavier Than the Heavens
The Academics Brains and Recreation Logics
The Strange Voice
The Chaotic World

Dedication

I dedicate this book to the United States and the other countries beyond and all the cities in the world today.

'When wisdom entered into your heart, and knowledge is pleasant unto your soul, discretion shall preserve you, understanding shall keep you' (Proverbs 2:10, 11).

Introduction

What are we seeing and what is going on in the world today? Where is the world moving toward? Oh world! People are confuse and do not know what to do.

There are noises everywhere in the globe. Many are dying without hope. What will happen now onwards? Who knows the evil hour? What can we do and what must we supposed to do?

Why are so many confusion and violence everywhere in the globe? Who is coming and what is He coming to do?

Will it be peace and what will this world going to be? Can this world will be free from violence?

Is there any good for this world? What will be the results? When shall we repent from violence's? Many people are confuse and did not know what to do? When will these violence's last?

There are so many questions in peoples mind wanting to find answers to their problem. Is there any hope?

What will be the end of this world history? Is there any solution for all these problems and confusion? Yes! Let's consider the following. Watch out!

Contents

1. The murky people

As if we are different in nature and different in stature. Our ways and thoughts are darkened and there is no soundness in our being. We have lost our identity as human beings.

Our nature has become as animals and many us behave as wild beast. We put the law aside and have left our morality for madness. We behave as if there is no God or the owner of this world. We are gloomy and jokers for sin.

We have lost understanding as human beings and have lost our dignity. Many of us behave as without mind and eyes. Sin has covered us and has destined us in prison with no keys to open. Oh! When will this nature change?

Who will rescue us from this situation? In fact, many of us are mad and are beast in behavior. Many people imagine evil every day and do things in madness. We are not clear as we should but dim in behavior.

Some of us lack sense and are mad in actions. Many of us love do evil than to learn righteousness. We have lost totally the image and the likeness of God. Our nature is serious in doing evil than well.

We love lies than truth and wish promote evil than good. We have lost understanding and have lost wisdom because of sin. Some of us are babies in mind but they are mature in age.

What will be the benefit of all these? How are we going to answer all these acts? What are we doing to ourselves? How will these going to end us? Our state as human beings has deformed by sin.

We have corrupted ourselves and follow vanities each day and night. Those who call themselves Christians behave like the devil. Some of them are warriors of darkness instead of light.

They cheat people with false doctrines and then deceive as light. Money has brought many peoples mind and they are control by lust of flesh. What will be the results concerning these things?

There are oppressions among the Christians. Oh! Why these things? Who is behind all these things? My dear, are you in the right position? When shall cease these actions and put away madness?

Now the world is leading the church leaders and some of them follow mammon of instead of God. Many Christians are confused because of false leaders and false doctrines.

It is hard for many to distinguish truth from the false. Many of us have taken God as their mate and doing things as they want. Others deceive and pretend as light killing people through greediness.

Some of us take fornication as nothing and support those who are doing same. Many of us lie and support those who do the same. Others disregard health laws and eat anything they like.

Many of us wear indecent dress and then cause harm to themselves and others in spiritually. It seems we have lost sense and mind to do something better for ourselves. Our nature has turn and there is no soundness.

We do evil; eat evil and dress evil. Our minds have become dark and it is difficult for many of us to differentiate right from wrong.

This is our nature today as human beings. Some of us are weak than weakness.

We are murky and dead in sins. Who can change our situation as human beings? How are we to receive this change?

What can we do to have this change? This should be our question and thought.

2. Different thoughts

Is there any possible way we can become one people with one mind? How will this be possible? Who can make us whole and change our situation eternally?

We came from one man and one mother, but with different mind; thoughts and attitude? Why different thoughts but one subject? What makes it so or caused this condition?

Why different views but the same lesson? In fact, we have big problem concerning us as human beings. Our nature has deformed through the sin of our first parents.

This is our situation as human beings who were created by the omnipotent God. Why perfect and omnipotent God but deform and miserable human beings with different thoughts and behavior?

Why different churches and teachings but one God? Why one Bible but different teachings? Why different religion but one God who created us all?

Why one savior but diverse followers with different views? Why one way; one truth and one life but different tracks; different truth and worship?

Why different attitude and behaviors but one Christ who is the same yesterday; today and forever? The confuse people; confuse world and confuse religions.

Diverse colors of people but from one source of birth and mother. As human beings, many of us follow their thought and what we think and suit their wish or like.

Our miserable state as human beings depends on what we think is good but not what God has said. We have put God's word aside and have trembled His Law our foot.

Many of us live with their sentiment and wishes think that it good to entertain it. Others take God's word for granted and think that, God does not mean what He says. There is no consideration in our moves and many of us do not fear God.

Our situation has missed up the ideas that we were created for. We cannot foresee what is before us and have missed the target of reasonable life. We are confused because of sin and then upset because of selfishness.

Now we have diversities of religion and teachings. Many people are disorganized and do not know where to step their foot.

The world is in the state of Babylon, where the one language was changed to many languages which dismantled their unity as one people. So, we are in obscured world and nothing is appropriate as it should be.

We are in chaotic and ferocious world; where misunderstanding grows each day and night. Many are confuse and overwhelming with needs and wants. Many of us die every day and lead others to dismay due to different thoughts and misunderstandings.

When will this situation last? Who will solve it for us? We are without proper peace and good atmosphere. Many of us do not know what to do because of miss up teachings and lessons.

We are in the complicate and gloomy world with different source of knowledge and opinions. One God; one world, but different kind of judgments of people with diverse attitude; One Christ but different followers of people with different teachings and views.

Is it well balance or not? What will be the consequence of these states of opinions? What will be the end?

3. The violence people

Oh! The world is now filled with violence of people. It has become dark and with a lot of misunderstandings among the people. Many people are greedy and do not fear God.

Others are with guns stealing and killing their follow beings. It is difficult to believe your brother and sister concerning matters of honesty. It is now difficult to live with honesty life because of us have corrupted their way of life.

Some of us as people are mad in behaving. Others live like senseless animals that cannot be control. What has happen to us as people and God creatures? Animals obey God and know their time.

Other creatures keep the natures law but human being does not want to obey the laws of nature. Many people of the world today have corrupted their life. Now lie is ruling the world and money is the king in all things.

Many seek money than their life and then want wealth than wisdom. Our way of life as human beings is dangerous than death. Many love to cheat than to spare and wish to kill than to save.

Our mind has been darkened and thoughts are always evil. What is going on and why these conducts?

It is now harvest time; the owner is now coming to harvest those dry grains. Bribes have increase and murdering's are on the tree leaves.

Is there any hope for the people of the world today? When shall we repent from our wrong doings? Many people have forgotten that there is a judgment before us.

We have case with the owner of this world. Who can escape the coming doom? You need to consider yourself and then consider your end of life. What answer will you give to the Master?

The time is coming that everyone will account for his or her deeds. What are we doing to ourselves as human beings?

It seems we have forgotten that there is a death penalty before each one of us. Yet, many of us are seeking wealth out of mind and carefulness.

Now some of the women are peak leaders of crime today leading men to sin grievously through deception and lies.

There are many scammers; many robbers, many murderers, many occults and cybercrimes all over the globe.

These led by lust of flesh and money which some of us are dying without hope of future. What are we doing to ourselves?

Oh! My brothers and sisters, this is not all but there is a great punishment waiting for us. Have you notice something? What have you observed? Shall we continue in this life of doom and curses? When will you stop these acts?

There are many things that we are doing that against God's law and nature. Many people have become the enemies of God because of their attitude. Many of us love the world and pleasurable things than God.

Some are following vanities things and not mind their life. Others cheat and support those who do so. People love murdering than loving and wish to kill than to spare. There are violence's everywhere on this globe.

There is no peace at all; yet wars and rumor of wars across the globe. Many people have lost their ideas and then live as empty beings. It is difficult to find those who are honest to duty and forceful of doing the honest work.

People seek money than knowledge and love vanity than life. Is there anything in these things that we are seeking?

Is there any life in it? What is the end of these things that we love than life? What is the profit in it when we lost our life?

4. Cheating people

When these actions will be ceasing? What is going to happen to those who engage in cheating their colleagues? Is the any profit in these things? What will be the end of these kinds of actions?

Now there are lies everywhere in this planet earth. People are cheating their follow brothers and sisters. Lies are growing every day and murdering's follow suit. Money has bought a lot of peoples mind and there is no favor in this earth.

People are wicked and do not mind to live in such a situation. Many love to do evil and also support those who did it. When shall you stop doing these things? Is this going to lead you into hell or will you repent from it before judgment?

Are you okay? It seems there is nothing worrying you but you love to continue doing evil? Is it right? It seems everyone in the world today wants to cheat his or her colleague.

Oh! Is this fair? Why is it so? It is a selfishness act that many want to entertain in their life. Many people love money than life and then want to cheat than to work for.

Some also has been bought by money and do not have liberty to control themselves but they are control by somebody's mind. Oh! What a world we live?

Politics has blind many people mind and some are control by politicians. Those who have positions rule those who do not and others are controlled by someone's knowledge.

Pastors are cheating; teachers are cheating, soldiers are cheating, police are cheating, medics are cheating and the rest. Who is faithful today? Who will stand for the truth or live honest life?

Many people are confuse and do not know what to do. Many appear as light and others pretend as good but they are cobras in the heart. Some are wearing sheep skins but inwardly are dogs.

There are false prophets cheating people and leading them to destruction. It is very sad to hear or see some of these prophets saying they are the men of God. Do not fear to do evil and do not mind cheat through selfishness.

Many of them are even wicked than the devil. These prophets have made others confused and do not know where to make a step.

They pretend as they love and want to support others who are weak, but they are murderers and tricksters. What will be the end of these things?

Lawlessness is all over in the globe. The world has become dark and the people who dwell in it are murkiest. This is serious and very disturbing. It is difficult find those who are faithful and honest to duty.

When shall we repent from all these things and change our style of living? It is sad and very sad to comment with. Our state as human beings today is miserable and disturbing.

The forces of evil are across every Conner of this globe; pushing people to sin and do other wickedness's.

Where are we heading towards and what do we want to do to ourselves? What will be the end of these actions?

Many of us deceive and cheat as well. Cheating kills and then dismantles the deeper knowledge and wellbeing of a person. It kills the person's ability and wisdom. It kills the spirit of gratitude and enthusiasm.

It support theft and disgrace the wellbeing of a man. Let consider our ways and doings, and then prevent disgrace through good works.

Let appreciate our belongings and thank God whatever the situation. And then stop cheating our brothers.

5. The differences of religion

It is sad and very disturbing that the world has dominated many kinds of religion but one God who created us all. What does this means and what it is so?

Why should this happen and what must we do and find out as human beings? It is so sad for us as human beings created by one God to be in this condition. What must we do about this situation?

We are confused as people of God and the sensible being of this creation. Where from these kinds of religions? Where are they leading us to and what will be the end? I am asking that, who created this world.

How many are the gods who created this world? Are heaven and the earth created by different gods or God? Is there any God apart from God who created the heavens and earth? Why different religions at all?

What will be the result of these religions? Christians have many believes and different names of churches. Muslims also have many believes and different kinds mosques. There are different type's doctrines and different interpretations.

There are so many churches in the world and different teachings but one God. Is there any effect about these kinds of teachings? What do these teachings are leading people to? Why different faiths but one Christ?

The world has falling and has become Babylon of old. People are confused and have missed the real road leading to life eternal. Who is telling the truth? And who is seeking the true God? Many are confused and have lost the road to eternity.

Oh world! Where from these kinds of lives that we are in? There are false teachings and interpretations among those who call themselves Christians. Others mislead people for money sake.

Some so called reverend of today are duping people for their interest through selfishness. Others are workers of the devil but pretend as light. Many people are confused and disturbed through the actions and teachings of these pastors.

There are disordered everywhere in teachings of the word of God. Many are disordered about these teachings and churches that are rampant in the world today.

Are there any reasons for these mushroom churches of today? Why is it so? Which of them are telling the truth? Who is following Christ in truth?

Money has blind many people's mind and they cannot foreseen the real truth for their souls. Their heart is far from God the Almighty but they near God by their mouth.

The reason of this many churches is based on one thing. They have rejected the commandments of God and then follow their own aspirations. Thinking that, it is right and acceptable to God.

Many Christians love to live by their own desire instead of the wish of God. They have made the worship of God so cheap and lawless. They have arranged principles of man for themselves instead of the principles of God.

Many of them follow their own ideas instead of the idea of God. They have put aside the law of God and the true teachings of His word. They have made the word void and useless.

They live contrary to the word of God and wish to follow the rules of man. For this reason that is why they have divided and have different mind and teachings.

If they will consider the law well, they will know the truth and the truth will set them free and make them one. God is not a dividing God but a unity and God of order.

What must be the object of Christians? Who they should listen to? What did they lack? Why are they divided? What they should know and learn?

Where from the mistakes that they have made? What must they do? If there is a division among them, it means there are different gods of whom they following.

What will be the result of this situation of their state? What they must know and do as Christians?

Let us not deceive ourselves on the bases of teachings and what we think it is good. But we should follow what the word is saying and does according the direction it lead us to. But not as we wish or desire; but what the word is saying.

So, the difference among religion is lack of knowledge concerning the truth God and the desire of our being that has caused this division.

Many of us are confused and do not know where they should put their faith. The churches are now obscured and disturbed through the reason of faith and doctrines.

Why one God but different opinions concern of His followers? This is a big question mark and sad to discuss.

Oh! Religious leaders of today, you need to find out of the reason of this condition and then make change for the sake of your life and then honor of God the heaven and the earth creator.

6. Different gods but one God

In fact, the most dangerous situation among the religions of the world is the kind of faiths they hold. Many of them are following the stones; woods and rivers which are lifeless and speechless.

It is sad to imagine the behavior some of them exhibit through their act of worship. Where from this situation and what will be the end? Is there only one God or different gods?

Why different followers and different faiths? Is God dividing? In fact, many of us have made their own gods and their worship. Others follow their thoughts and wish that suit their lust.

We have made world disordered and abysmal. Our sins have broken us and many of us have lost their wellbeing. Many pastors deceive by their tongue as they are speaking new tongue. But I ask what the new tongue is and what is the old tongue?

Do not deceive yourself; neither others, yet you cannot deceive God. It seems there are different tongues apart the tongues that God has given to us.

I want to them to know that, there is no new tongues accept what God has given to us. And there will no new tongue apart from what we know and speak by different kinds of people and their tongue.

So, any tongue that is new is a foreign tongue speaking by foreign man. Any tongue that has no meaning is not a tongue or language.

It is a deception and meaningless speech or noise. In fact, the world is now confused because of difference of languages;

religions, faiths and cultures. It is difficult to understand some certain things in the world.

The world is in the state of Babylon where people were separated by languages. But people are confused not because of languages yet because of religion. Religions of today have made the world into deep trouble.

Religion has destroyed the beauty of the world, and the real understand of nature and creation. Many people are confused because of religion. The ruin of the world today comes from faiths or believes of the day.

Why because people do not want to obey what God the creator of the heaven and the earth has said. Many of us want to pay homage for the devil instead of God.

Our first parents made him ruled over us and accepted his word instead of the word of God. This has brought the difference of religions and worship.

Many of us do not know whom they worship or serve. It is the devil who made all these deceptions and difference in believe.

Now, my dear sister or brother, I want you to think of it and know who you are following and to find out the religion you are holding. In fact, Satan has misled many people in the world today concern these religions.

Religion have made the world confuse and disturbing. Who will consider this and then find out the real one that leads to the God the almighty. There are different religions of people but One God.

What must we know and consider? What will be the results of all these religions? There many voices out there that is difficult to find out the real one. These are the voices of religions that have made the world confuse and difficult to make a decision.

Who is telling the truth? What must we use to test the truth?

Note and consider this message: to the law and to the testimony if they did not speak according to this, means there is no light in them. You need to consider the kind of religion you are following and then watch out.

7. Misunderstandings

The world is in trouble day and night; people are fighting for positions. Others are greedy in doing everything.

Where are we focusing, and what are our problems? Many of us are confuse and do not know where they should attend.

There are noises everywhere in the globe. Many people are crying and others have loss hope. There are wars and mix-up in all areas of the globe. Some are dying through hunger and poverty.

Others are suffering through diseases and stress. Many people are crying through oppressions and servitude. There is no peace in the world but wars and rumor of wars.

The world is in trouble every day. Marriages have broken and the children are suffering through broken homes. Money is now ruling the world and those who do not have are suffering.

Many people are making money unlawful ways and others are killing their colleagues for money. Some are cheating through selfishness and lying for favor. It is difficult for others to get employment because of bribe.

There is no truth in this world. Money has bought many people's mind and they are control by another person opinion.

Others are move by the instruction of giants and the politicians. Oh what a world we live, money rules, talks and control people who are weak and do not have faith in God.

There are misunderstandings among people in the world. Even Christians are fighting each other and there are differences in their teachings.

Others find it difficult to decide through these differences among Christians in their doctrines.

We are in war and there is no peace at all. There are darkness's all over and misunderstandings throughout the day.

This is our situation as people in the world. Many of us do not fear God and do not mind to keep the laws of nature.

Things are not in order but brutalities are going on each day. The world is confused and there nothing moving on well, everything is in chaos.

We all need to make change and do something that will bring our progress. There are arguments between people each day and night.

Others are fighting on lands and properties. What are we seeking for and what do we want to gain? Oh what a world we are in, all things are in trouble and people do not have peace. The states of many people are horrible and abysmal.

There are drug addicts; smokers and strong wine drinkers. There are many mental abusive of people who are leading many business firms and hold high positions.

It is sad that, many of these people are leaders of many nations. People who do not know God and neither have the knowledge of God. The whole world is in danger for the sake of these people who are now leaders of our nations.

It is a serious matter that needs to be considered in a second time. Due to this kinds of people have made the world inconsistent and dismantled. Oh world when will this state changed and who can make it better?

Troubles come each day and terrible things happen at each moment. People fight for power and money and then kill innocent people every day.

Oh what a world we live! There is no peace or calmness in anything we do. These are cause by lack of understanding and correct knowledge of God.

What will be the end situation of this world? What is going to happen in the next coming days? What decision have you made my brother? Why are we in this condition? What transpired?

8. Different actions but one people

Our ways and life are the same but with different actions. Our conducts as people are contrary to one another, but with the same flesh. We are one flesh or people but with different thoughts and mind.

We are from one father and one mother with the same flesh and blood but with different attitudes. Our state as people has a big question mark and it's difficult to explain.

Our attitude is questionable and there is no action without secrete. That is we act through the secrete things we have plan to do.

The world is turning round and there are days and night born through this move. Our ways and life are different from each other but with the same body and blood.

Is there anyone who can solve this problem for us as people? Why chaos every day on the globe? Our nature as human beings has a big question but the problem is the answer that we all need to know and have.

Our mission as people has changed and many of us are confuse and did not know what to do to survive. We are different but with the same blood and flesh.

Our situation as human beings has entirely changed and our ways of life are always in danger. Many of us follow their thought and what they think is right, instead of the principles of God.

They have leave God with different questions and then living with their own wish. It seems we are not from one hand or one creator? But as if we were created by different gods.

What is the main reason of these differences? What this behavior or attitudes? Why some of us are criminals and others are weak? Why some of us are greedy but others are not?

Why some of us are thoughtless but others are not? Why some of us are thieves but others are not?

Why some of us are meek but others not? What is the main reason of actions and where are they comes from?

There is something we should know about these differences? What will be the result of these actions? What reward will these actions will receive?

In fact, we have a lot to count and many to guess with. What question must we ask ourselves of these behaviors? Where these actions are leading us to?

Who is behind these actions of me? What will be the end of these actions of me? We need to ask ourselves of these questions.

Our nature today witness what the Bible declare concerning our first parents sin. It makes clear that there is a devil that is behind all these difference of attitudes and actions.

So, main reason of our difference was cause by the devil. He made us confuse by his lies which our parents followed.

This has made the differences of religions; the differences of doctrines, the differences of teachings, the differences actions and the others. We are all confused as people and the world. What must we do and know about our condition today?

Where these actions and differences will lead us to as people? What will be the reward of each one?

We need to find the solution concerning these problems. Where will you stand? Who do you following? Who is behind your actions?

9. Is this the idea of God?

No, but what transpired? In fact, God created us like Himself. We are his image and likeness but not with one blood or body. The idea of God for us became void when our parent obeyed the devil.

The whole world changed and corrupted through disobedience of our first parents. They became naked and miserable through the acceptance of the devil into their home.

They became the agents of the devil instead of the agents of their Creator. The world was created out from nothing and it was perfectly designed for man and his wife.

The world became their permanent home and gift for eternity. They were perfectly made and good for reason. The purpose is to live and development for eternity as the second home of God.

The atmosphere was good and comfortable. There was no death or sickness. Peace and happiness reign the world was beautiful to behold.

There was no waste or decay of anything that were created. Man was made to live and create like God.

The trees, animals and the others things that we see today were made for the good of man. The man was made to live eternity with good health and wealth. We are the joy of God and friends of good angels.

We are the crown being of the creatures that were made and the ruler and the manager of all creation. The world was ordered and very good. It is design to suit purpose with profit and hope for today and future as well.

There was no useless or thing that has no reason or purpose by which it was created. In the beginning God created the heavens and the earth. The world was formless and empty.

Darkness and waters are in deep of the surface and there was no light or day by which one can live in. it was formless and void but with deep darkness and waters all over the surface.

God cause light to appear and made days and darkness positions. That is, He separated the light from the darkness to make differences of their positions by which it must rule.

He commanded the waters together one place and to let the dry ground appear. For six days He created the world with abundance of things with good appearance and useful.

He made man and his wife with His likeness and image. The world was in order at that time and fair. There was no death or sickness, yet joy and welcome atmosphere.

Where from these calamities; death and sickness? Special home was made for man and his wife. The Garden of Eden which was filled with fruits fit for food. Yet there was tree called knowledge of good and of evil in the midst of the Garden.

The tree was sign for their continuous obedience and secrete for their progress. The man and his wife must obey what they has been instructed concerning their life.

But the sad story was that, the man and his wife disobey what they has been instructed not to eat or touch. They could not sustain their dignity, yet envied and lust what they has been forbidden.

This step destroyed the whole idea of God and brought us death; disease and calamities. Our confusing and difference as people today, was made through our first parents disobedient.

Shall we continue in this today as they did yesterday? Where shall we stand, when He comes? We are our own risk and enemy that destroys God's idea for us.

10. Why confusion among us?

Can bad tree bear good fruit? Can water and oil be one substance with no differences among them? Will dog and cat live in one cage with no war? Two roads cannot be used at the same time with one car.

Neither good nor bad can live together. Two rulers cannot govern one city or country, neither one king can ruler two different countries; unless the king captures the other country through war.

Why confusion among us? Why difference of people in behavior and attitudes? Why differences of churches and doctrines? Why groups of religions with different thought and minds? Many of us have become confused.

Others do not know where to turn or go for rescue. Our minds are darkened and ways corrupt. We are confused duty to our situation as sinful beings.

The devil has stolen our minds and has deceived us through lies and charms of the world. We are in war with good and have become the enemies of God. Everyone is looking for money but not life.

We love beauty than knowledge and love thoughtless than carefulness. We follow thoughtless than thoughtful and wish to cheat than to support. We are obscure as people and did not know where to turn for rescue.

Sin has degraded us and has confused us as people. Our nature love death than life and our ways are evil always. It is difficult for us to do good duty to our sinful nature.

We are all heading towards trouble instead of peace. We are confused duty our sinful nature and have lost the right way.

Darkness has overshadow us and we cannot see ahead to move to the place where our souls can be rescue.

We are fighting each day and night and some of us are dying without hope of salvation. Many people have missed the right track and the correct knowledge that will save their life.

Some of us are cheating the weak ones and others are bribing their colleagues. The world is in the fire and many are suffering through poverty.

There are bad teachings everywhere on the globe and those are not well learned are confuse and misled through these false teachings.

We are confused because of our differences of mind and thoughts. We are confused because of power and cheating. We confused because of many religious bodies. We confused because of false doctrines and teachings.

When will these things be over? Who can solve these problems for us? What will be the condition of tomorrow's life? We are confused because of wickedness.

We are confused because of bribes. We are confused because of misunderstanding. We are confused because of wars and rumor of wars. We are confused because of differences of interpretation of the bible teachings.

We are confused because of politics. We are confused because of cultural differences. We are confused because of differences languages and continents. The world is confused because of today's knowledge (science) and other matters of life.

Oh the world is confused duty the people who are living on it today. Is there any hope for the world?

What will be the end situation of this world? How have you prepares yourself for coming doom? Will you be saved? Where shall you go, when the world destroy?

11. When shall this nature be over?

Many people have been misled by today's knowledge or arts and sciences. Many of us as people are disordered and overwhelm duty to many thoughts; mind and teachings.

There are many errors in today's so called science. This has made many of us as people are crush. There are many experts in errors, but people do not know that they are in error.

There are teachings of today that have made many people mad duty it's false and meaningless. Others are confused duty to competition of today's knowledge.

The world has change and there is nothing good as it was from the beginning. Our first parent's sin has brought a lot of miseries to the world. We are confused duty to our sins and nature of life today.

Languages has disintegrated us duty to our sins behavior. We are in error state and our doings are errors. Many of us cheat one and another and then keep on murdering others every day.

We are in verge of the world and it is almost in the stage of destruction. The time is far spent and there no more days ahead of us.

Many countries are fighting each and the other seeking for power. Others fight on themselves for positions and properties.

We are in the war and groaning for money sake but not in for salvation of souls. Many of us die everyday duty to fear of wants and others die through mistakes.

Is there any hope for our situation that we are all in? When will this hope coming? Who is our hope for all this problems? When will He come? What will He do? Who shall be save when He comes?

Oh who shall rescue us from all these problems? In fact, there is coming day when all these troubles will cease and the world of today will change for the better.

These troubles will one day cease and the things of the world will take its proper cloth again as it was from the beginning. There is hope for this world and the people in it.

Christ is the hope of this world and He is coming to us and to change this world again to it first state.

What we see today will be forever end and it will not come to mind again. The confusing will be no more. Sickness will be no more. Pains will be no more.

Poverty will be no more. Oppressions will be no more. Positions will be no more. Oppositions will be no more.

Politics shall cease and cheating will forever end. Stealing will be no more. Murdering shall cease and the bribe will be never heard off. Wars and rumor of war will no more hear off. Gambling and other cheating games that make unfaithful money will be end. The garb between rich and poor will end. There will be no differences of languages but one people with one king and one language.

Haughtiness and partiality will come to an end. Beauty and pride of people will be stop. There will be no kings; presidents, judges, doctors, lawyers, engineers and the others that we see today. There will be no death or killings of people.

Christ will come and solve all these problems and trouble forever and ever. It is our hope that, all these troubles will one day end.

But the peak thing that all of us must ask; do and seeking is faithfulness to duty as the Master seeking to have from us. All this chaos; confusing and other things causing our ruin will be end in a moment.

12. Who can solve these problems?

Our situation today is painful, we are in trouble every day and people are dying day and night. There is no joy and peace in the world.

There are sufferings and death; sickness and pains. Hopes of people are gone and there is no cheerfulness. We also always heard and see sadness.

There are unseen agonies mending people life into wreck. These are situations of our lives as people on the globe. What shall we do and what can we do about it?

It has come to us, and what will we do? Oh my dear, we are all in trouble and dying day and night. It is seems there is no hope in future of our lives.

When shall these things cease and who can solve it for us? When shall we wait for and what time will this end?

We are fighting and we are dying moment by moments. This is our situation as people in the world. Death; sickness, pains, chaos, poverty and other matters have come to stay and no one can escape of this things.

Many of us are crying; others are wailing, some are groaning and others are in sorrow wanting or seeking for relief, but there is no answer for their problems.

We are in trouble and the way is tough to pass through. Who will rescue us from all these wailings?

When will that person comes and help us in these matters? This is hard life for us and difficult to go through. We are confused and do not know what to do? This is serious and difficult to explain.

Our condition is tough and bad to guess. It does not have any cure or balm that can heal. This is terrible and testing that needs supernatural to solve.

The mind is sick, the heart is weak, thoughts are always evil and there is no soundness in the mind. The whole head is sick and the body is burning with sins. We are in the peak of trouble and the peak of sins.

We need savoir on this matter and comforter about this situation. When shall these continue as it is? This matter cannot be solved by any human being, whether by his power; by knowledge or by might.

There is no balm for this situation of our being that has been corrupted by sin will be healed. So, who can solve this sin nature for us? Who is that person?

How did He solve it? Why can He solve it? He took our nature and He was fashion like one of us and overcame evil and it matters.

He was God but counted it as no reputation, yet took form of a servant and became one of us with the same blood and flesh. Who is this man? It is Christ Jesus the son of Mary; the son of God and the son of man.

He is our peace for He has broken the wall of separation and made it peace. He overcame sin and death, and He is alive forevermore. He is the one who can solve our problems and the death penalty that is before us.

My dear human being, we have a lot to count and to face. This life is not all but there is a judgment before us as being. Everyone will account for his or her deeds and then receive the reward suit to it.

Let us consider our ways and doings; there is no time for jokes, no time for gambling's, no time for wickedness and no time for positions and properties.

Let us keep in mind that all these moves will end. Watch out and look up to heaven for your salvation comes.

13. Why greediness today?

Oh what a world we live! Men have corrupted their ways. Many people love money than life and then cherish pleasure than God. We all have gone astray and each one for himself but not the other.

Everyone is looking for his or her own benefit than other and others seeking to be leader than servants. Many others love to cheat than to help. Greediness is all over the globe and the lies is the ruler of the day.

There is no consideration of each person and lies are been promote by bribing. Oh what a world we live? People love money than work and love bribe than wisdom.

There are a lot of challenges among us and then envying the fortunate who have been work faithfully for their produces. Oh what is going on the world today? Who is faithful?

Who is ready to stand for the truth? Who will live sufficient life and then accept his or her condition each day?

It is times for us to fight for truth but not money; to stand for modest but not abundance of things.

When the man again the whole world and then lose his life, what is profit he will gain? What are you searching for? Why are you so greedy? Let consider our situation today as human beings.

Many of us as pupil cheat and mislead others who are weak because of selfish life we intend. Our away of life has become deception in all our doings. We cheat and pretend as good people and mock others by our lies.

What have you considered in your life? What do you do to the others around you? Are you greedy or selfish? This is the end time and everyone must watch out for his or her salvation. We need to keep in mind what is before us. Everyone is going to face his or reward due to the work done. We are all hurry to get wealth as quick as possible. But what will be the end?

Let consider our doings and then change from wrong acts. What are we doing to ourselves today? Cheating and murdering one and another.

Greediness cannot bear good fruit but leads to death. We must accept whatever we have and then give thanks to God. Do not love the world; neither things of the world, the world and the things are passing away; yet the one who love God shall live.

You must accept your condition and things you have is all seasons. Do not be hurry to get wealth but wait upon the Lord and then be strong.

Put away envy and do your honest work; it shall be well. Do not force yourself to be rich; yet gather it little by little to keep your-self from damage. It is better to be poor and live peaceful life than to be rich and then ruin your life.

Do not hoard up through greediness but accept your little belongings and then stay safe and peaceful. Greediness comes by envy and it makes fruit through selfishness.

Do not follow wealth but wisdom to fulfill your mission with honest and then harvest abundant life. Let us keep in mind that everyone will receive the reward of the deeds exhibited.

Do not compare yourself with others, neither considers their wealth. Yet keep yourself and accept your belongings. Now it is time to keep yourself well and then do away greediness and then save your soul from eternal doom. Do not look to others concerning their wealth, but look to God and be saved.

14. The peak time

The time is far spent and days are now left a few. We have reached the top of the mountain and there is no way to descend or come down. The world has reached the peak point and the things are now falling apart.

There is no future again for those who hope in today's world, but future for those who hope for the coming one. When will you come out from your wrong doings? Why are you wasting your time on the fake things?

There is no time for jokes and no time for envying. We are in the horrible state in the world history today. The air that is blowing, show the end of today's world.

Many people are seeking for high positions and abundant wealth. There is no care in the way that people live; that is many people live as they wish and think is their rights. Others cheat and think it is okay.

There are wars and rumor of wars. Challenges are all over on the globe and false reports are rampant. There are noise successes everywhere which many people think is a blessing to own houses and luxury cars to proof your acceptance of God.

This has no basic proof concerning blesses of God. So many people are seeking wealth instead God and their future position.

Oh! Will you mind to change your thoughts and your ways that seems good in your sight? There are a lot of wickedness's going on. Many people do not mind to get wealth through killings of weak ones.

Robberies are all over the globe; stealing and killing at the same time. Many people are seeking wealth unlawful ways and also killing innocent people.

There are corruptions everywhere; false teachers and prophets allover. People are confused to live and others are broken by false messages. Many others want to live a cheap life and make money without law.

The world leaders are hoarding up belongings for their families and their own interest. Selfishness has gain position than selfless.

Many people are drinking wine and make merry without consideration of honest life. Oh world! When will you consider God and your life? Why loving world than your life? When shall you repent from your wrong doings?

Have consider the coming age? Where will you stand at the end? Do not climb the tree with your back. Means do not live by the way that seems good in your own sight.

Yet, live according to the setout regulations and then prevent damage at the end. The world is running out; there are noises everywhere, people are fighting for positions.

Now many people want to live anyhow and eat anyhow and drink anyhow. Some of us want to dress anyhow and then live without consideration.

Money has bought many peoples mind and some of them are control by wine. Darkness's are across everywhere and people love bribe than honest work. Many people pretend and deceive by their acts.

Some of us pretend as Christians but follow the devil directions. False doctrines are growing each day and night. People love lies than truth and then cherish jokes than awareness.

There are many fake pastors and prophets today making money through greediness; pretending like Christ followers but denial of the true worship and godliness.

But they have many followers; praising them through their lies. Some Women are their supporters praising them by senseless acts and lacks of knowledge of God.

Many people have taken worship of God light and then doing what they think is right at their own estimation. There are many jokers in the world today; thinking that they are worshipping God in truth.

So many pastors mislead people by their false message. Others too deceive to gain money. There are a lot of wickedness's going on in the world today. Oh! What are you looking for?

Why are you wasting your time on the goods of the world? Here is not our home; the world is going to the end.

We all need to behave well and then keep ourselves from corruption this world. We are in the probation time and the time of grace. Let us watch out and keep watch for we do not know the time of visitation.

15. It is a test time

Now is the time of grace and time of salvation. We are in the probation and there is no time again. We are in the test time and probation. The world is now dark and it is in sad condition than ever before.

There are violence's everywhere on this earth. Now, many people are wicked than ever before since the entry of the sin. Many people do not care their life. Others keep on in killings their brothers.

Theft has increase and murder follow suit by those robbers. Wickedness has hoard up and lie displays in the air always. People do not fear God again and mind mercy.

Bribes are license for the increase of the wealth. There is no law working on the on today in people's lives. Many people love cheating than working for.

Many of the youth are now fornicating day and night. Bad dressings are all over causing harm to the mind of many people.

Sin has increase than ever before and many people are bathing it like water. These acts are calling us to meet our Lord in air. It is a test time and trying moments for all human beings.

For this reason many people will be discourage because of rampant murdering. Now knowledge has increased but many people lack understanding.

All these things are calling us to be ready for the Master turn. It is a test time, who will pass this test world then win the crown. Many people's mind has polluted and darkens; by which there is no light at all.

Today's murdering are the signs of the end time. Many people do not understand the reasons why it is so. Do not be confuse about these matters, it must come to prove the true saying of Christ.

The devil wants many people to be on his part and then deceive many as he can. The world has changed and it is going to destroy. There are dominant of wickedness of the globe today sounding everywhere.

Money is the king ruling on everyone's mind and then controlling people to do foolish things. Selfishness has grown to it height, but there is no proper improvement as which they want.

Why? What is the end of these things? What is the benefit of it? All these things are testing of our faithfulness to God.

It is a hard times and the testing of our faith in God. There are wars and rumor of wars pointing to the peak time of today's world situation.

What have you considered? How prepared are you? When shall you repent from your wickedness? Will you continuing in your wickedness? Thief comes to steal and kill; our situation in the world today is horrible.

What are we hearing and what are we seeing? Killings are all over and people are dying without hope. We are in the testing time. There is no mercy in the world today.

Many people are mad in mind because of money. But it is a testing time; we are all in balance, weighing us to see our fitness and honesty. Who shall stand? Who will be fitted at the end? It is a test time.

The fear of Lord is out from men and there is no fear of God again. Everyone is going to receive his or her reward at the end according to the work done. It is a test time, and there is no time again. What will be your portion? Will you mind?

16. What are you doing?

What are you waiting for and what are you doing? Have you considered your doings? Do you mind your actions today? Are you on the track? Do you follow your mind or God?

What are your actions? Are you faithful? If you look around, what do you see? What is your action towards that? Oh! What are we seeing today and what is going on?

Will you continue in this? When will you repent? Why are you still misleading people? Why are you still lying? When will you stop deceiving? Will continue in fornication? When will you stop stealing?

Many people do not know when they will be paid through their work. What salary are they going to receive? Will it be fair or not? But it depends on the work they did. You will be paid according to your doings or work.

So, why don't you do the right work or thing? Is what you are doing fair or truthful? What have you considered or noticed? What do you think?

Is it true that you did it according the requirements? Oh dear. You must know more than you know and consider your direction.

What is your aim? Where are you focusing? Will it be better for you? What have considered and know? Will this be better when you try?

Is that dress good to wear? Will that food help your health? What is your mind? What do you imagine? What will be the end? Do not pretend as you know everything, but let others teach you. Be a learner and teacher as well.

Do not raise your head up or despise others opinion. Come down and do your best as it suit the occasion. Learn to share and keep on sharing with others.

Do something for recognition with good report. Stop cheating in work with others and then do your honest part. It is not good era, yet it is a trying time with dangerous hours. Is what you are doing good or bad?

What have you noticed? Many people have turned their back to God and doing what they wish. Others prefer lies to truth and wish to cheat than support. They love bribe than sacrifice and then deceive than beauty. They love by mouth but fails in action.

Others love money than life and love wealth than truth. When will you continue in these things?

Oh keeper! What is the time now? Why are you joking in these bad times? What are you doing? Is it right or wrong? Will it help you?

Many women have taken this world into their bosom and doing a lot of horrible things. They have regardless their life and respect. They have putting their eyes on their back and moving forward without eyes.

Means they are intentionally doing wrong as without law in life. What are you doing? Will this be good results? My sister, do you know what you are doing?

Do you know the end? Will you be accepted by the Master? When will you repent from those actions?

Do not take the world or things of the world into your bosom. Yet manage the life according to the regulations or laid down rules, and then prevent your life from ruin.

What are you doing? Means are you on the right path or living as you suppose to live? If not, change from those wrong doings and then save your life from eternal doom. It is not good time; will you consider and then stop harming yourself at the end?

17. When will you return?

Will you continuing doing evil? Where will this end you? When will you return or stop doing wrong? Ask yourself who is controlling me? Is what I am doing right?

What will be the result? Where I mine going to stand? What will be my reward? Many people keep on doing evil and others are murdering with their mouth.

There are shadows across the sky and darkness is taking over the world. Many people are crying and some are dying without hope. What is coming to this world?

Is there any hope? What will happen in the next hour? Who can tell the outcome? It seems you still regardless the time and you do not mind what are coming.

Shall you continue in these things? Be patient in life and never rush at this moment. But prepare yourself always and seek the truth. When will you return?

Do you want to follow wisdom or foolishness? What have you decide? Where are you making your direction? Will that journey help you?

Why don't find out the end of this journey you have decided? You have gone far please; return it is not too late.

It shall be well and there is hope, only if you will return from your wrongs. It is not late at all; He (Christ) is waiting for you and wishes you well. Do not look at the waves, you just return to Him.

He knows the thoughts and the plan He have prepared for you. It is of hope and great expectation. Change your style of living and build yourself well.

Return, oh! Backslider son; your Father is calling you. He is afraid for you and love to save and comfort you. When will you return? Do not wait for long, He is calling and waiting for you.

Though, many people are seeking for wealth and belongings. Others are killing for properties, but what will be the results? It is not late, come oh backsliding son.

Return and come home son; you are dear to Me, I die for you and have considered and chosen you! When will you return my dear? You have been favored and loved. You are dear to Me.

I have loved you with an everlasting love, said the Lord. You are always present in my eyes. Do not fear and be not dismay, I am always with you till the end of time. You are dear to me and wish you well.

This is the word of God to us. We have made this world sad and uncomfortable. We all are doing what we like and regardless the laws of God. You do not fear to sin and does not mind to do wrong.

Now the world is filling with violence and darkness all over the globe. The time is far spent and days are no more. Oh! How long will this continue and how long will you repent? When will these last?

Do you fear God? When will you return? We love money than wellbeing and wish selfishness than development and good character. It is time for you to return from wrong doings and change your steps.

We are in the end time and anything can happen. We do not know what is before us, but we can prepare for any outcome. Make good steps for your feet and turn from those evil works and then fear God. When will you return?

18. He is coming

We are almost home; the King is coming to reward everyone according to his work. He is coming. Have you prepared for His return? Will you be accepted when He comes?

What will be your reward? You need ask yourself about these questions. The world is now in the balance, weighing to find out the weight of violence it had.

Whether it's must stay or not. What will be the results? We are on border of the world; waiting for rescue and comfort. The wind that is blowing is the sign of His coming.

Look, He is coming on the cloud and everyone will see Him. The world will be silent about Him and all the people will be amaze of Him. Why many wickedness today?

Why rampant robberies today? Why too much cheating all over the globe? Why greediness all over the world? Why killings and lies everywhere on the globe.

Why war and rumor of wars everywhere in the world? Why misunderstanding in all the group of people in the world? Why false prophets everywhere in the world? All these things are callings us to meet the King in the air. He is coming! The world has reached the highest height of the sin.

Darkness has covered all the face of the world. There is no light to see ahead, darkness is all over the world. Many people love money and others are greedy in seeking wealth.

What do you see and what are you saying about it? Will people continue in wickedness? When shall all these things last? What are you doing? Violence upon violence and killing upon killings are going on.

When shall all these things cease? These are the signs of His coming calling us to repent form our wrong doings. In fact, those things that are going the world today are calling us to prepare and meet our Lord in air.

These should not be surprise but it must be a lesson to us. This shows the condition of this world and what the sin of our first parents has brought to us.

Everyone must prepare and to be ready for the bad day. For what we see and hear are calling us to be alert. Is your salvation dear to you? How serious are you in this time of crisis?

What are you doing to save your life? Will you be able to come out? The world has reach in the deepest stage in sin.

It is time for God to do way sin and punish those who are involved. What brought flood in the Noah's time? Now the Spirit of God is ceasing from striving with men, because they are flesh.

Our days have shorting and there is sound again in our members. Our conditions as human beings are horrible and it needs disciple through the acts of God.

Now the wickedness in the world today is great. The fear of God has gone from men and there is comfort in the world today. In fact, our condition in the world today is terrible.

People love to sin than to do well and now madness has fill up in the mind of men. Women has destroy the beauty this world. Many of them wish to do wrong than good.

They have made this world dark and gloomy because of their wearing and appearances. They have block good knowledge and understanding and have made world unfair.

When will they repent from their short comings? Now men follow suit and wish them on wrong doings. Violence are all over the world and people love to sin than to do well.

Oh! When shall these things end? Who will consider his or her deeds and then stop wrong doings. Oh world! Christ Jesus is coming to pay each work done.

What have you notice something? What are you doing? Will you continue in these wrong acts? In fact, these days are dangerous for men and all those who dwell on the earth today.

Our thoughts are evil continuously and our doings are evil every day. Who is ready for Christ return?

Who have prepared to meet Him? Look, He is coming with the cloud and His Angels are with Him. Now, it is time for us to repent from our wrong doings and set straight path for our feet.

We are not in good times, anything can happen? What is your goal? Where are you focusing? Keeper, what is the time now? It is now probation.

We are in the time of grace and there is no time again? What will be your reward? Oh keeper! Prepare and meet your Lord. Will you consider this message?

What are you doing about it? Is your life dear to you? When will you repent from your wrong doings? Remember, we are in the probation time, and there is no time again. Prepare to meet your God in air.

19. Is it a sign for something?

We have come to the borders of this world history. All things are calling us to prepare and then meet our Lord. It is a sign for the coming judgment that proving its tragic it will be.

Now you can see the impact that this disease has brought. Have you prepared to meet your Lord coming? Will you stand? What will be your reward? We have spent about 95 percent of this world history and we do not know when our Lord will appear.

He already told us that He is coming soon, which means it will be happen at any day or time that we are not aware off. Everyone must be ready to meet Him. He is coming on the cloud and everyone will see Him.

In fact, this pandemic is smallest among the coming ones. There are a lot to come. What is going to happen as He has already told us will be terrible? Those things that are coming to happen will new ones which have not happened before since the world exist.

Let's consider what Amos said about the day of the Lord. Read;

18Woe to you who desire the day of the LORD! For what good is the day of the LORD to you? It will be darkness, and not light.

19It will be as though a man fled from a lion, and a bear met him! Or as though he went into the house, Leaned his hand on the wall, And a serpent bit him!

20Is not the day of the LORD darkness, and not light? Is it not very dark, with no brightness in it? (Amos 5:18-20)

No one shall escape this day, every will receive his or her reward. There is something approaching that testifies the sign of the son of man. We have case with Him to resolve and then receive the reward that suits it behave.

Do not joke this time in your life but be ready and meet your Lord. The pandemic is the sign of the coming one; calling us to raise our heads and look at the King of Kings and Lord of Lords.

The will experience something terrible from this disease and the lesson will be tough to stand with. Read Amos 6:9-11 read;

9Then it shall come to pass, that if ten men remain in one house, they shall die. 10And when a relative of the dead, with one who will burn the bodies, picks up the bodies to take them out of the house, he will say to one inside the house, "Are there any more with you?" Then someone will say, "None." And he will say, "Hold your tongue! For we dare not mention the name of the LORD."

11For behold, the LORD gives a command: He will break the great house into bits, And the little house into pieces.

Many people will die through this pandemic, will you and I live? If yes, what will be the next? If no, what will be our reward? This lesson is not just a lesson but it is reward which testifies the end means of everyone.

This is for the entire world witnessing the coming doom of all of us at this age. It is a time for us to practice justice and make straight path for our feet. To repent from our wrong doings and then seek the welfare of others. Read this text and take note.

Take away from Me the noise of your songs, For I will not hear the melody of your stringed instruments. But let justice run down like water, And righteousness like a mighty stream. (Amos 6:23, 24)

It is time to turn from iniquities and then do good and justice like running water. It is time to look up for your salvation. What is coming is great than the greatness.

Will you be please the Master? We must seek good and not evil, then to have life for our souls. So the Lord God of hosts will be with us, and then have mercy on us as He has spoken.

We need to hate evil, but yet love mercy and establish justice in our gates. It may be that the Lord God of hosts will be gracious to us who will remain in this pandemic that has come to all people.

It is a sign warning us to prepare and meet our Lord. It is time to keep the sayings of the Lord. The time will come; the word of the Lord will be scarce. Note this text;

"Behold, the days are coming," says the Lord GOD, "That I will send a famine on the land, Not a famine of bread, nor a thirst for water, But of hearing the words of the LORD.

They shall wander from sea to sea, and from north to east; they shall run to and fro, seeking the word of the LORD, But shall not find it. (Amos 8:11, 12)

Many things will be calling us to be ready for the son of man appearing. All that we need to do is to prepare for His coming. So, this coronavirus is calling us to ready for Christ second coming. Let's read the message from Christ mouth and take note.

Therefore you also be ready, for the Son of Man is coming at an hour you do not expect.

"Who then is a faithful and wise servant, whom his master made ruler over his household, to give them food in due season?

Blessed is that servant whom his master, when he comes, will find so doing. (Mathew 24:44-46)

So, it is better for us to be ready for the master return. Then, it will not take us surprise when He returns. Everyone must seek the Lord and live.

We are going to face many tribulations in this time of world history. Everyone must be alert for that; there is more coming harder than what we are facing now. Read Mathew 24:29-33

29"Immediately after the tribulation of those days the sun will be darkened, and the moon will not give its light; the stars will fall from heaven, and the powers of the heavens will be shaken.

30Then the sign of the Son of Man will appear in heaven, and then all the tribes of the earth will mourn, and they will see the Son of Man coming on the clouds of heaven with power and great glory.

31And He will send His angels with a great sound of a trumpet, and they will gather together His elect from the four winds, from one end of heaven to the other.

32"Now learn this parable from the fig tree: When its branch has already become tender and puts forth leaves, you know that summer is near.

33So you also, when you see all these things, know that it is near—at the doors!

We should not take it as a normal thing but we must be ready for those horrible ones that are coming. This coronavirus is the opener for others that are coming. It is warning us to prepare and then get ready for the coming doom.

You need to watch out and then keep watching. It is time to meet the Lord in air. Are you ready? Have you prepared?

Note; Blessed is that servant whom his master, when he comes, will find so doing. Assuredly, I say to you that he will make him ruler over all his goods.

But if that evil servant says in his heart, "My master is delaying his coming," and begins to beat his fellow servants, and to eat and drink with the drunkards, the master of that servant will come on a day when he is not looking for him and at an hour that he is not aware of, (Mathew 24:46-50). Be ready!

20. What must we learn from it?

The world has owner and the laws that govern it movement. The creatures of this world must live according to the regulations govern it. Man is the crown being above all creatures made by God. It is not God intention for a man to suffering or die.

But through disobedient man became a death being. In fact, all that man can do depends on the power of God for him to perform well. Without Him man cannot do anything appropriate or well that suit the standard which God demand.

Whatever plague we see today comes by disobedient that our first parents did. The development of sin has reached the standard that needs punishment. It is now time for God to do away sin from the entire universe.

But He is warning us to repent from our sins and then come to Him for salvation. But those who are wise know the time of their master returns. These people have notice it and have prepare themselves for their master return.

This pandemic is calling us to be ready for the coming doom. So, it is not just a sickness that has come upon the world but it is giving us a sign concerning the end of the world.

If anything bad happens, it is for our lesson to take note and repent from our wrong doings, because there is a terrible judgment coming. The world needs to face penalties because of sin that we have committed.

Why this pandemic at this time? Why it has come? In fact, the world today has developed in terms of advancement since the man came as a living being. But what this development has brought to us as human beings?

What do we see concerning this advancement of the world today? In fact, sin has advance through this advancement of man knowledge. It is good that we have developed but is it for? What have we reached through this development?

What benefit have this progress has giving to us as beings? What did the Bible has said about this development and which time will it happen? Let's read from Daniel 12: 1, 4, 9, 10, 11 read;

At that time Michael shall stand up, The great prince who stands watch over the sons of your people; And there shall be a time of trouble, Such as never was since there was a nation, Even to that time. And at that time your people shall be delivered, everyone who is found written in the book.

4"But you, Daniel, shut up the words, and seal the book until the time of the end; many shall run to and fro, and knowledge shall increase."

9And he said, "Go your way, Daniel, for the words are closed up and sealed till the time of the end.

10Many shall be purified, made white, and refined, but the wicked shall do wickedly; and none of the wicked shall understand, but the wise shall understand.

11"And from the time that the daily sacrifice is taken away, and the abomination of desolation is set up, there shall be one thousand two hundred and ninety days.

We are in the end time and all things witness. What is going on today witness what the prophet Daniel said in his book? It is truth that we are in the end time of this world history? Yes! It is totally truth, all things testify.

The increase of knowledge is key note that witness the end time of this world history. Many shall be purified, made white and refined, but the wicked shall do wickedly and none of them shall understand, but the wise shall understand.

Those who are wise know the signs of the times and they are ready for any outcome. So, we must be ready for the coming doom.

Each one of us will face the penalties that are before us. It is time for us to repent from our sins. Now the increase of knowledge of today's world has made us deceivers and fraudulent.

We have developed through knowledge of good and evil through technology of today. Each one of us deceives and cheats the other. We take it as nothing and even joke about it. Many of us think that, it is a normal thing to cheat your brother or sister.

Now, many people want to make money unlawful ways but take it as nothing. Others bribe to increase their wealth. There are many things that we are doing to break the Law of God but regardless of in penalties.

The wise shall understand and keep themselves from it. But wicked will not understand and shall do wickedly. Many shall be purified and made white and refined. Here, this pandemic is purifies others, whiles others has taken it as the normal thing.

We need to watch out and then repent from our wrong doings. Else, we shall destroy with the wicked.

This coronavirus has come on it time warning us to come out from Babylon (disorder) and other false acts.

Let's read Mathew 24:15 "Therefore when you see the "abomination of desolation,' spoken of by Daniel the prophet, standing in the holy place" (whoever reads, let him understand),

It is now time for us to understand the abomination of desolation that Daniel the prophet spoke about standing in the holy place. This is a lesson for all of us alive in the world today. Everyone must take it serious and stop his or her wrong doings.

This disease has come for our aid and salvation. It is announcing to us the coming doom which no one can stand. Let us thanks God for this pandemic, for it has come in it due time calling us to prepare for the bridegroom coming.

It is also letting us to regard the health Laws which gave to us concerning our diet and hygiene. It is teaching us and warning us to come out from wrong doings and then preparing the wise to their Lord in air.

There are more to come, horrible than this one. We all need to be vigilant and then keep watching the doors. Else, the thief will take us captive unaware. It is for our aid and redemption. Will you mind?

For Good Living and Knowledge Gain!
B. B. S. LIFE BOOKS.

The Chaotic World

Also by Bernard Benson Sarfo

The Fact Among Facts (1st)
The Fact Among Facts

Standalone
The Youth Murderer
Be Original Not a Copy
The Christians Science or Scholarship
Precious than Paradise
Habit makes future
A shelter from storm and rain
The Science of Life
The Strongest Lion Knockback
The Perfect and Inspiring City
Above Hope, Faith and Love
The Hero's Brave Decisions
The Weakest Among Plants
The Hero's Brave Decisions
Doing Above The Ability
The Wisdom Beyond Power And Greatness

Heavier Than the Heavens
The Academics Brains and Recreation Logics
The Strange Voice
The Chaotic World

About the Author

Bernard Benson Sarfo is an acquainted architectural designer and a motivational speaker.He is a gifted teacher who continues to motivate and encourage many.

Read more at https://www.amazon.com//author/bbslifebooks.